Life Wires

Kristine Sihto

Life Wires

Kristine Sihto

TinkerInk
2019

First Printing: 2018
This edition first printed 2019

ISBN: 978-0-9942984-0-9

Kristine Sihto
c/o TinkerInk Publishing
20 Jackson St
Eagleby, QLD, 4207

www.kristinesihto. com

Illustrations by Kristine Sihto.

Cover photography: Tree Lights by Nicolas Raymond.

Ordering Information:
Special discounts are available on quantity purchases by corporations, associations, educators, and others. For details, contact the publisher at the above listed address.

Dedication

To all the stormy eyes who brought
so much conflict into my life

These poems are your children.

Contents

Innocence

Beginnings

A clean page,
A fresh start,
A new day,
A young heart.
Dewdrops shining
In the morning sun.
The promise of springtime.
Something's begun.

The Little Horse

Today I was a little horse.
My mummy said "Behave,"
But horses don't know people words
So I stayed a horse all day.

Mummy didn't tell me "Giddy-up",
She didn't say to woah,
So all day long I just ate grass,
And yum! I loved it so.

Mummy says that horses
Don't sleep inside at night.
They get shut up in stables.
They don't have a bedtime light!

I think I'll be a little girl,
'Cause that's a fun thing too,
And I'll find another thing to be
Next time I visit the zoo.

Kristine Sihto

The Little Penguin

I have a little penguin.
He's naughty as can be.
What's wrong with my little penguin, you say?
He wants to fly, you see.

He sees that he has feathers.
His wings are there alright.
He is a bird, and rightly so,
He's ready to take flight.

He jumped off of a building.
He's lucky he didn't go splat!
"No more learning to fly," said I,
"Penguins can't fly and that's that!"

Next thing I knew, a parachute
Came for my penguin by post.
What is he going to do with that?
"I'll fly!" I heard penguin boast.

So he donned his trusty parachute
And from a skyscraper jumped.
But my penguin didn't really fly;
He just landed with less of a thump.

And now my penguin's disappeared,
I don't know where he is.
I hope that he has given up
This crazy idea of his.

Today I got a postcard.
My penguin, he's no fool.
He must really want to fly,
He's going to pilot school!

I'm proud of my little penguin.
He'll go straight to the top I'll bet.
How many penguins do you know
That can fly a Jumbo Jet?

Lump

My lump is a wonderful furry thing,
All cuddly, soft and warm.
My lump is as gentle as can be
And would never do me harm.
My lump is a lumpish, humpish thing,
I love my lump, I do,
And because I'm nice and treat it good,
My lump, it loves me too.

Little Lion

I loved that cuddly toy of mine.
Some kids choose teddy bears.
Predatory, even then,
a tiger shared my cares.

I was still so little then;
one cat was like another.
I called him 'Little Lion'.
"It's a tiger!" said my mother.

Little Lion went everywhere
a toy tiger could be dragged
until he wore out totally
and his fur was torn and dagged.

I haven't seen Little Lion for years –
he was packed away in a box
by my conscientious mother.
I hope he isn't lost.

I'll find my Little Lion,
even though I am full grown.
He'll take pride of place
on the highest shelf in my home.

I know that he will love it
when I put him up on show,
for where else for the loyalest tiger
that a growing girl could know?

Cat Dreaming

My cousin is a hunter,
Far away in distant lands;
Not caged in pleasant suburbs
Or confined to human hands.

They say that I am lucky,
I am wild and I am free,
But I dream of far off jungles
Of ancestral memory.

I try to be more like them,
I hunt when I'm in the mood,
But it can never be the same
If I don't hunt for food.

My cousin is a king.
I'm commoner than that.
The Lion may be free,
But I am just a cat.

Childhood Sensuality

Raspberry cordial,
Thick, honeyed syrup,
No water, coating my tongue
With its cloying seduction.

Glace cherries
Straight from the fridge,
Sticky on my fingers,
Eaten out of sight.

Dancing in night-time rain,
Naked in the yard,
Cold pinpricks drilling
Through the layers of my skin.

Hidden in a closet,
Smelling violet perfume
Upon black velvet
That lies against my cheek.

Pricking fingertips so gently
With my mother's silver pins,
Running hands through needles
In her sewing drawer.

Smelling sap that's trickling
From the gum tree's bark,
Hugging close the roughness
Pressing hard beneath my hands.

Cotton Candy

at the edge of the world
the sky is ablaze
the clouds
set to fire by the sun
slowly sinking to the horizon
above
young gods play at carnival
and chew on pink
cotton candy mists
they colour the sky with
pastel dyes
and ignore the flames
in the distance
as the glow fades
one by one
we see the gods' eyes
wink open
and stare down
at a sleeping earth

Tri Fold

The full and yellow moon
hangs bright overhead
as I dance
naked.
Candles flick red light
across my skin.
I rejoice
in her glory,
clothed
in her shadows,
nourished
at her bosom.
Maiden.
Mother.
Crone.
She lies within me.

The Birth of the Green

Glimmering teardrops
cascade from the face of the sky,
falling soft
and gentle
upon the fertile earth.
The soil wakes,
lives,
breathes;
and so the green is born.

Kristine Sihto

Brightly Grows the Grass

Drab grey, drab brown,
Dead grass on the ground
Waiting dryly for the rain,
For summertime to come again.

Spitter-spat the raindrops fall,
Wetting grass and trees and all.
Green is shining through at last.
Brightly, brightly grows the grass.

Royal Bluebell

Pretty blue flower,
Shaped like a star –
Your delicacy
Shows how fragile you are.
Know that I won't pick you
For I know you will die,
Your petals will close
And will droop as to cry.
So I leave you grow wild
By the side of the street
So you can give pleasure
To the people you greet
Nodding your head
To the blue of the sky,
In clusters you ripple
As I pass you by.

Kristine Sihto

Tree

She stands tall,
clad only in the sun,
stretches her arms high,
whispers her wisdom into the wind.
Many years now has she stood here
patiently waiting.
For what?
Only she may know.
Her feet have sunk deep into the soil
and from this spot she will never move.

Ibis

Ibis stands in black and white,
Feathers ruffle in his fright,
Looks at me from on the rim
Of a common refuse bin,
Dips his beak in search of what
Scraps he sees we wanted not.

It seems a sad tale that I see:
This bird who once majestically
Ruled this country's swamps and fens,
Reliant on our garbage bins.

The Game

I have a little game I play
As I walk down the street.
I look at all the faces
Of the people that I meet.
I imagine there's a mirror
With their face instead of mine,
And I am in their body,
And I'm feeling rather fine.
And if I looked in the mirror
Every day upon that face,
Would I think that they were ugly?
Would I hate them for their race?
And if I were walking down the street
And I met up with me,
Would I notice this one person?
And, if yes, what would I see?
Because everybody's beautiful
In their own special way,
And we all look in the mirror
Each and every single day.
And if you just see the colour,
If you just see the skin,
You will never see the person
Who is beautiful within.

The Artist

A glance into your eyes
Can show me worlds I've never known,
And my mind can feed upon
The precious seeds that you have sown.
The flower that will bloom from them
When they are fully grown
Is unparalleled, more beautiful
Than any now full blown.

Rock

The wall is all.

The wall and me.

Her dusty face
pressed to my cheek,
and I, so close,
cling to her skin.

Her hard and warm
suffuses all.

      step. scrape. click. reach.

I trace her lines
and carefully
I lay the course.

My breathing rasps
inside my head.
My heartbeat pounds
in fingertips.

And once again:
      step. scrape. reach. shift.

My belly burns
on sun-seared rock.
My muscles pain.
My fingers grip;
and I exist
in only now.

I ever close
cling to her skin.

Life Wires
 step. step. reach. scrape.

The wall is all.

Seduction

Corvid Blues

Corvus orru melted me
with glistening blue eyes
they looked into me
just like you do
and left me
crow black

The Oldest Waltz

Dawn follows Midnight,
Slipping softly by his feet,
Creeping ever closer
Until at last they meet.
Dancing hand in hand,
Around about they twirl;
Dancing for eternity,
This ageless boy and girl.

Mermaid

My heart hurts.
Her beauty calls me,
Beckons blue-green
Like sea whispers.

My heart hurts.
Her tinkled laugh
Like shards of glass
Falls on my naked ears.

My heart hurts.
I long to enfold her,
Become her,
Hold her.

My heart hurts.
Curve of neck,
Crook of elbow,
I ache for her skin.

My heart hurts.
Siren desire,
Lost in her ocean,
Lost in her cool.

My heart hurts
For selkie,
Kelpie,
Mermaid fair.

Self-Loathing

She stands at the bar,
smiling and flirting,
eyes locked with the lost soul
That pours cash from deep pockets.

She uses it all,
leans so that cleavage
spills from her dress,
all the while fascination
at each word he says.

Later in the alley
short skirt lifts,
rum sweet breath
mists soft upon the face
of the stranger who is lying
within her sacred core.

Be damned if I don't love her
for the slut she's always been.

Sizzling Summer Sirens

The bus buzzes,
heat and voices in the sun.
The bus thunders to a stop
and a beauty,

> *Goddess of fire,*
> *red silk and sweat.*

walks,

> *seductive strut*

sits next to me.

> *Coyly she raises her eyes to meet mine.*
> *"Hello, lover," slides sweetly*
> *from her red, pouted mouth.*

Her long hands

> *her long fingers,*
> *red tipped nails,*
> *creep slowly up my leg,*
> *longing to plunder*
> *the wet and warm,*
> *longing to touch*

turn pages on a book,

> *Sizzling, sultry,*

cheap romance,

> *cheap sex.*

Her long, pointed tongue
licks lips parted slightly.

> *Her long, pointed tongue*
> *licks my lips.*
> *Hot breath mingles.*
> *Her long, pointed tongue*
> *ravages my mouth,*
> *invades the space,*
> *flicks at my teeth.*

A trickle of sweat
moves softly down her brow

> *bosoms.*
> *The trickle of sweat runs between her breasts,*
> *perfect globes of flesh.*
> *The sweat sticks between us,*
> *slick, sticky, tickly trickles.*

Her arm rubs mine
in the closeness

> *in the privacy*

of the tiny space we share.

> *Her arm rubs my breast*
> *in the privacy*
> *of the tiny space we share.*
> *Her hand cups my breast,*
> *tweaking nipple*
> *until hard and firm.*
> *Her mouth cups my breast,*
> *her tongue taunts and tweaks*
> *my hard, aching nipple.*

Her hand cups my sex,
finger seeking
hard nipple,
seeking the core,
seeking the pleasure,
seeking the listful, blissful, glistening nipple.
"Oh," I moan.

"Oh," I cry.
She looks at me, puzzled.

> *She looks at me, satisfied,*
> *sensual,*
> *sexy.*

I don't explain.

> *I am in too much pleasure to speak,*
> *so much that*

She rings the bell for her stop.

> *I hear bells ringing.*

The bus shudders to a stop.

> *I am still shuddering.*
> *"I'll be back soon," the lips,*
> *red, glistening, murmur.*

She walks

> *shimmies,*
> *sways,*

off the bus.
On steps a beauty,

Goddess of ice,
cool, white,
linen and lace.

walks,

glides,

sits next to me.

Snake

Slithering serpent silently sighs,
Looks at the world with more than just eyes.
Myriad colours blaze scales on the skin,
Belying the coolness that lies just within.

Sinuous serpent slides over the sand,
Travels the tunnels and trails of the land,
Seducing the stranger who watches the glide,
Making me want to be snakelike inside.

I want to taste the world on my tongue.
I want to languidly lie in the sun.
I want to live in the wild and be free.
Shimmering serpent, reside within me.

Scylla

I am Scylla,
Waiting, watching,
Hungry for those that dare pass by.
I will snatch up your men:
Your sons, your husbands,
And they will feed my dreadful appetite.
They will not flee.
I can appear the loveliest of creatures
If only you care to look.

The Poet

His words are sharp with steely teeth
Which rip and rend what lies beneath
My worn facade. His words are bold.
They grab my heart and take a hold.
His words amaze. His words become
My centre and my total sum
Of all I need. He captures me
With verbose capacity.
I fill with woe. I brim with ire.
His words fill me with such desire
For unknown he. Oh, how absurd!
My passion burns for but his word.

Ode to Mr Moose

An orange spotted car and a pink flamingo
twisted in a place of straight and dull.
Craig leaped to save the day
from being dull and boring
just like every other day.
I hate American accents,
but this was music to my ears.
Goth scares the local straights.
I don't wear black anymore
because they sucked
the rebellion
out of me.
I want to be free
like Craig.
I want to display my weird
like Craig.
Craig is beautiful
because he is not afraid.
A man who merely passes through
can be brave.

Met In Passing

It seems quite strange to think of you,
A man met in passing, and I barely knew,
But while the opportunity to know is there
There's a place in my heart you already share
With those I love. How do I explain
How thought turns to you again and again?
A smile, a touch, a look, an embrace
So precious to me I could not replace.
Your voice, like an ember, has set me aflame,
But all I have of you is a name.

Leo

He is the one.
The Lord of the Sun.
A magic man,
my mystery man.
So carefree,
so closed to me,
yet what does he see?
He sees my all
as into his fiery depths I fall.
He reaches into my soul
and swallows me whole:
him I would like to know.
I don't fancy my chances.
There are only glances
into the vast darkness of his mind
that makes me blind.
But I know all that counts.
The one thing to which he amounts.
When all is gone, one thing shall remain,
unchanged,
still the same:
His name.

Guitar

he shines when he plays.
the music pours out of him
like liquid light
dripping from his fingers,
pooling,
slowly spreading
about him like shadow inverted.
he shines when he plays,
strumming,
thrumming,
golden glow
shaved from the strings,
ringing,
bringing me to my knees.

Sleeping Angel

I saw you sleep today;
The peaceful angel out of place.
The tension drained from body,
Contentment on your face.
Beautiful, your absent smile
Relaxed, but only hidden,
The lines around your face to show
It's truly been well lived in.
The line of brow now still, serene.
Now slack the cheek and jaw.
Here and now, while you're asleep
The light of God is yours.

Kristine Sihto

Storm Clouds at Dusk

grey-blue of pale slate
at any other time
but you turn to me
storm clouds at dusk
when you smile
the black abyss they surround
widens
engulfs me
and I am left tumbling
down down
deep into fathomless depths
where it is warm
where there is joy
where my heart longs to be held

The Twentythreeness

he is beautiful
like the number twenty-three
so odd and primal
in a double-digit way
no evenness or
smoothly suave
his lumps and bumps are joyful
he bounds exuberant through my discipline
I crave attention
from his sky-blue gaze
some day

Kristine Sihto

Fire and Dust

Light gleams and dances in your eyes.
When you smile, nothing can disguise
The beauty in your open face,
Your spirit, and your honest grace.
But underneath the open smile
A hurting heart lies all the while,
Shy of being burned again,
Wary of the naked flame.
The world is cold and I am warm;
I'll shelter you from wind and storm,
Enfolding you in loving arms,
Protecting you from any harm.
Yes, there is the roaring fire,
Burning pillar of desire,
But that, to me, is only dust.
I simply need to earn your trust.

Reflections

The white of the moon lights its place in your eyes,
Perfection a delicate glimmering beam,
Reflection of otherwhere so it would seem.

But the moon but reflects the light of the sun.
Without sunlight, her beauty would never be seen.
Reflections in your eyes, a sparkling sheen

Reflecting the joy that lies in your heart,
Reflects only love and devotion, and see!
I look in your eyes and reflected is me.

Absent

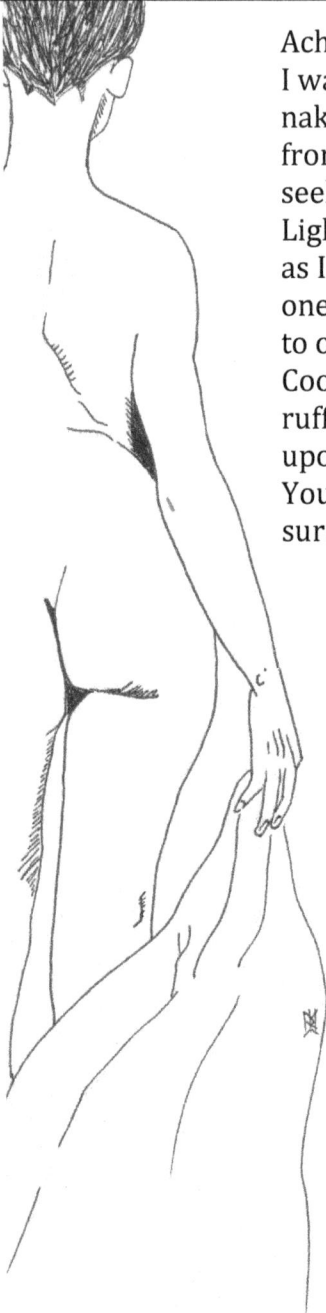

Aching for your return
I walk
naked
from room to room,
seeking.
Lights die in my wake
as I move
one step at a time
to our bed.
Cool cotton sheets
ruffle
upon exposed flesh.
Your scent
surrounds me.

Batu Caves

Alone, I climbed three hundred steps
to reach the Batu caves
and in Murugan's temple
your image stood with me
and whispered, "So majestic," in my mind.

Hands on hips, and looking up,
you pointed out the trickle there
of water, there some green
where a tiny patch of sunshine
could bring life.

And I realised four thousand miles
was not enough to end
the hold you have inside of me
called love.

Gravity

do you recall
as a child
the swing
in the park?
push, push,
'til you swung as high
as the tops of the trees?

then
that moment
when gravity
realised
that you could fly like a bird
unless it took hold.

for just that moment
weightlessness
clawed and gnawed
in your gut
with precious
fierce
gentleness,
then you fell
back
along
that pendulous path.

now
because of four words
here I am
weightless once more.

gravity,
let me fly

First Kiss

Let me sink down
Into that dark rainbow of oblivion.

The internal beat of the flames
Fills my ears
With a rushing loudness,
Exploding in my stomach,
And – pop!
I am reborn
A child of passion and wonder
And the world is new
Again.

Relation

North

when I step in the room
my compass points to you
incontrovertible
a lodestone draw on me
I feel you when you're near
unerring cardinal

Captivated

you speak
my heart stills
you laugh
i feel thrills
you whisper
i cry
your tears fall
i want to die
you rejoice
larks sing above
you captivate me
i am in love

Fall

Gently I fall onto the bed
Into your waiting arms.
Gently you fall into my heart;
I'm captured by your charms.
Your smile enraptures, titillates,
Traps me in your eyes.
Your lips entrance; your fingertips
Draw forth my longing sighs.
You fill me with your loving need.
To me you're all that's true,
So I have fallen, here I'll stay
Trapped in love with you.

Tongue

Much more than mere fingers,
More than simple touch,
We intertwine.
Soft lips.
Smooth teeth.
Rough,
Wet,
Tendril of taste.
I show you my love.

The Hidden Place

There lies a space inside of me
Where no one dares to go,
The place that holds my other-ness
That I never dare to show.
A face of dark intensity
That captures all my sin;
A place of pain and hatefulness
That I hide deep within.
Sometimes I feel I'm all alone,
That no one shares my fears.
And is it pride that makes me think
That no one sheds my tears?
But everybody fears sometimes
The monsters deep inside,
And everybody feels sometimes
That urgent need to hide,
And everybody feels sometimes
That insecurity,
And I feel a little better
Knowing that it's not just me.

Grey Eyes

Grey eyes of cold fire,
a glistening flame,
rest on me a moment
then move once again.
They tear down my walls,
see into my heart,
they take my emotions
and tear them apart.
They make me feel things
that I've never known
and then they are gone.
Once more I'm alone.

The Journey

I have walked many moons,
Travelled many paths,
Scaled many mountains
To reach your door.
Now I am here
I see the sky is bluer,
The birds sing songs
I have never heard,
And there is more beauty
Than I could ever imagine.
I am tired.
Footsore and weary.
I thirst.
I hunger.
And you say,
"Come!
Travel yonder roads,
Scale yonder mountains,
For there lie beauties
Neither of us have seen."
There lies a path before me
That I must walk.
There lies a mountain before me
That I must climb.
I am weary.
I am footsore.
I will stumble and fall
At pebbles in my path.
But I walk on
With a smile,
For you walk with me.

The Flesh Of It

I love you in the pit of my belly,
    where my spine meets my ribs
    and my bones hum your name.

I love you in my brittle skin,
    where thoughts of touch
    set my world aflame.

I love you with each single hair
    which stands to reach
    with tender yearning.

I love you with my eyes' embrace;
    to your visage
    it keeps returning.

Saturday Morning, 9AM

Oh, would you please shut up?
I just want to sleep in.
But somewhere in the distance
A power saw makes its din.

Oh no, the next door neighbour
Has started mowing his lawn.
I rub my eyes and stretch a bit
And give a great big yawn.

Perhaps if I close the window
The sound won't bother me.
But wait, no use, in the next room
Someone's turned on the TV.

"Maybe I should just give in,"
A voice says in my head,
But as I rise, another voice –
"Honey, come back to bed."

Nimue

Merlin,
Your steel-boned hands,
Magic weaving,
Weapon wielding,
Bloody, dripping hands
Have touched my bridled, beating heart.

O, loyal dog,
He took your best,
The years splashed gory
On the mystery of history's page.

Your sword-crowned king,
Tempestuous,
Incestuous;
Why could you not see
How it would end for him?

He took you from me,
Demanded your all,
For what is love?
Just me.
Just my soul.
Years unreturning,
Years full of yearning,
You touched my bridled, beating heart.
You formed my jealous, zealous heart.

He shall not have your all,
Nor your best.
I've waited so long,
I claim the rest.
Come into my crystal world.
Claim one moment.

Claim my love.
That moment shall last eternally,
And together we'll shut out the
world above.

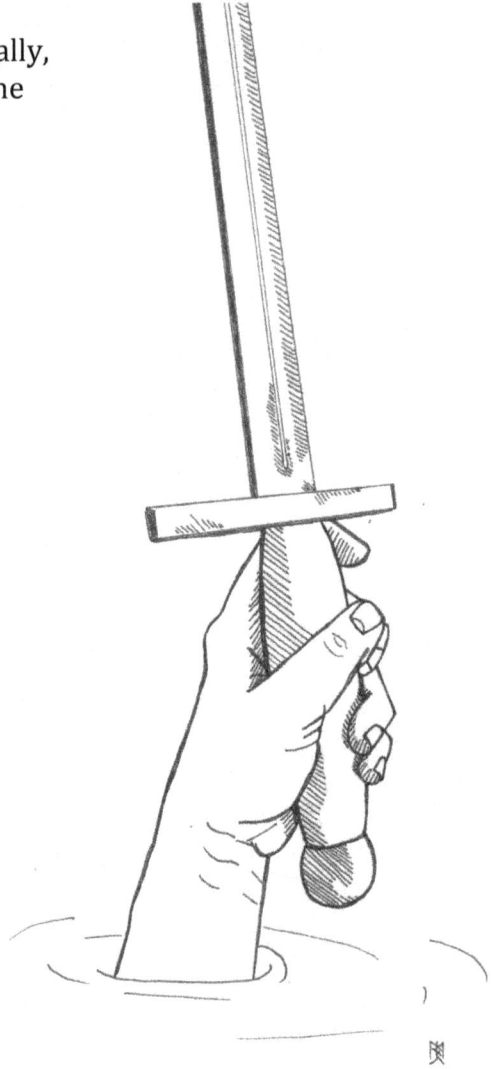

Resignation

He is going.
He is leaving.

In the nooks and crannies of me
lie the tiny bits of dark
that his light never erased.

Pain.
Grief.
Lonesomeness.

In his absence they expand again
to fill the growing void –
a person-shaped expanse.

He is going.
He is leaving.

The tiny bits of darkness fill
entirely too much of me –
spills out every orifice.

Eyes.
Mouth.
Everything.

My eyes are running over. I shut
my mouth to stop the pain
infecting more existence.

He is going.
He is leaving.

It itches and it stabs my eyes,
swells in my throat to choke me

and pain hitches my breathing.

He is going.
He is leaving

and I will be alone.

The Man in My Bed

The man in my bed is gone.
The emptiness continues, on and on.
Nightly he sleeps no longer here.
Alone I am left to deal with my fear.
He will return! There will be calm!
The seconds tick by on the watch on my arm.
My strength he took with him. I cannot sleep.
I lie in the dark counting ethereal sheep.
The darkness struggles on and on.
The man in my bed is gone.

Kristine Sihto

Love and Death

If love hurts this much
Let me die.
If love hurts this much
I'll pass it by
If love causes
This much pain
I won't stand up
To be hurt again
If love hurts this much
Love is a lie
So now that love has hurt me
Let me die.

The End of the Marriage

So it comes to this,
messages on the refrigerator,
impersonal,
dates and times,
who rang when,
what they said,
in the least possible words.

Dissolution

Bleed

Torn apart,
a piece of me
disappears.

I long to be free.

A devil is taking
a part of my soul,
ripping me to shreds.

I long to be whole.

Leave me alone!
I don't have what you need.
Take it from someone else.

Leave me to bleed.

Undone

Self fades,
It disappears to Who-Knows-Where
becoming Once-You-Were...

Now, what was Self,
or Ego,
is

> My Wife
> My Mother
> My Daughter

> My God

What happened to

> Me

Or even

> I

Maybe the words were so small
that nobody thought
they mattered

The Mask

I collect masks.
All over my house
Holes for eyes
Stare.
But nobody notices
The ones that I wear.

Emotional Baggage

hearts break
like glass –
loud,
shattering into thousands of tiny shards
that cut everyone they touch.
some wounds show immediately.
the blood spills to the floor
in a crimson cascade.
but some wounds don't show
until they are touched,
cutting only later,
and the pieces that you forget to pick up
can even harm someone
who was
never
on
the
scene.

Labels

I never wished to be

> The Shrew,
> The Harpy,
> The Leech,
> The Sponge,
> The Clinging Vine,
> The Weeper,
> The Wailer,
> The Ball-and-Chain,
> The Cross-to-Bear,
> The Stick-in-the-Mud,
> The Pain-in-the-Ass.

Instead I became

> The Jack-in-the-Box

who jumps up
smiling
every time
even though I may be

> Broken.

Late Night Movies and Forgotten Dreams

Late night movies and forgotten dreams
Gaze upon me, and "Awake!" they cry.
I, now woken, silently sigh,
For morning sun illumes my face.
Exposed I am, within the light,
Naked now to those with sight.
My mind with broken mem'ry teems.
I long for cool, concealing darks
Where those afar cannot see my masks,
For there I can pretend a grace
That in the light I do not possess.
I there can hide my emptiness.

Judas

See me, the one lost,
Searching for the one who stole my soul.
This is a grey place,
Hazy,
Where none can see
Beyond the end of his nose.
He is there, perhaps, only a footstep away,
But I am blind in these mists,
Blinded within my madness.
Where is he?
This shroud cloaks me
In an endless, emotional death.
His uncaring silence
Crucifies me.

Silence

The still, calm silence
invades,
cutting deep into the soul
like the knife,
hovering
above the vein.
There is only Now,
eternal,
absolute,
final.
They will cry,
but only after
eternity
is ended.
Now, they do not see
the still, calm silence
choking me.

Memento Mori

Your name is forgotten.
I am a bad person.
Something in my head says
It started with P…
I am a bad person.
You were my first girlfriend.
It shouldn't take much to
Remember your name.

    Petunia?
    Paula?
    Pandora?

It wasn't Pandora.
You gave me Jim Steinman.
Pandora's Box played on
That stretched-out cassette.
I am a bad person.
I lied and I told you
'You are so beautiful'
To your plain face.

    We cuddled.
    You talked.
    I listened.

You spoke of the one who
Had been here before me
And how you'd adored her
And prayed she'd return.
I held you and kissed you,
Your salty wet teardrops
Coating me with sadness
That I was not her.

Life Wires

     I listened,
     Quiet,
     Supportive.

And there, while I kissed you,
You put your arms 'round me
And said, 'Have you done this?'
I said, 'You're the first.'
You spoke, as I kissed you,
Of how it was painful –
That you couldn't love me –
Your strength was too low.

     I offered.
     Your face –
     Grimacing.

You spoke of your cancer
That ate out your insides
And how all the surgeons
Had taken your bowel.

We woke in the morning
Still huddled together.
Your fridge could not feed me.
It held only beer.

     My stomach
     Growling,
     You just drank.

You took me for breakfast
At ten in the morning
To sit with the drunks at
The bar down the road.
You taught me to play pool,
To line up the balls and
To pocket them – sometimes

(I wasn't that good).

> Packet chips,
> Shots and
> An eightball.

We stayed there six hours
With pool and with drinking,
Awaiting your friends, then
You introduced me.
You called me 'Day-tripper'.
'Straight-girl experiment'.
I slipped out quietly
While you did not see.

> Patricia?
> Penny?
> Pamela?

I let you slip quietly
Out of my life because
You could not love me
Because I was bi.
I am a bad person.
Your name was Amanda,
With Terminal Cancer.
We lasted two days.

> My tears fall
> Loud in
> This moment.

You live in my memory,
Two days of happiness,
Two days of sorrow,
A lifetime of guilt
That I couldn't stay there,
That my needs were greater,

Life Wires
That I didn't hold you
And watch as you died.

  I wish you
  Were here
  With me now.

I don't know your gravesite.
I don't know your last name.
You gave me Jim Steinman.
I'm still bad at pool.
You were my first girlfriend.
Your name was Amanda.
Two days of guilt-tripping
Live on in my heart.

Kristine Sihto

The Breakdown

everything was black and white to you.
you never gave an inch
to understand the grey world that ruled me
like a tyrant.
you loved me enough
that when i said i would take my life
you called someone
who took me to another grey place.
but, when i returned, you left me alone
to be with my children and my fears.
i sat, trembling, waiting for your return.
you did not understand.
your world is black and white.
there are no in-betweens.
there is no place for me inside your stark reality.
it is easier to let you go
than to make you understand
how real my grey love for you can be.

Teen Dreams

Grey white, misty, newspaper crinkle memories
Of your smile, right-handed, lopsided,
Snapshots of each moment.
Your sparkled laugh is muffled
Behind the mirrored glass of time.
The fog of years lies heavy.

I see still images,
Your eye, wrinkled at the corner in joy,
Your hand running through your fringe,
Unconscious that movement, practised often.

Were they ever real?
Or just a mirage
And I am stranded in the deserts
Of the present.

There Was A Time...

There was a time I knew all his vital stats.
Middle name, birthdate, phone number.
His Arien temperament and Aryan looks
Piercing me blue with his deep sky depths.
There was a time I could recognise him
Simply by watching his left elbow,
Keloid scar pronounced upon white flesh.
Eyebrows black, hair blonde, unusual combination.
His legs were hairier than any other man's.
There was a time. Now long gone.
Years of long alone.
There was a time...

The Mirror Girl

I watch the mirror girl at night.
She always eats alone.
She snuggles in her favourite chair
And sits by a silent phone.
The mirror girl looks sad, as if
She's cried a million tears,
And sometimes she looks scared, as if
She has a million fears.
I don't think I've ever seen someone
Like her in all the world,
And I really think I'm better than
This lonely mirror girl.

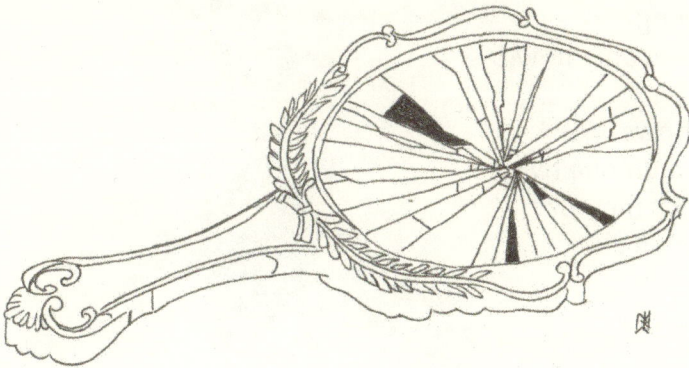

Now is the Time

Now is all I have.
There has never been a better time to say
"I am strong."
There is only now.
And when the world deals me blows,
I say "I am weak,
But only now,
and now,
and now."
I only need now.

With each second that I hold on
It leads me closer
To the second when I will be fine.

I am all I have.
I am weak,
But I am strong.
Because I have only now.

I count the nows
Ticking them off one by one.
I call the nows memory.
I survived them all.

I am only now.

Metamorphosis

The dreamer dreams within his bed,
The demons lie within his head.
The dying dies within its tomb,
The embryo breaks from its womb.
It feels the sun upon its face
And it knows this is its place.
Break away the outer clay
That makes your life seem drab and grey.
The ugly stone you see inside
Is just a diamond trying to hide.
Some will dream their lives away,
Some will hide, but I will stay
And face the promise each day brings
And revel in a thousand things
And pity dreamers who never know
The love you feel when you learn to grow.

Junction

"Wordsmith," you called me,
"What word do I need?"
I blinked.
I pondered.

My mind traversed alleys
In search of your context.
A thousand wrong choices
presented themselves.
In that moment of failure
I wished, for an instant,
to see past that curtain
and into your mind.

"I need time!"
my brain clamoured
for your opaque intention.
I cannot write your truth.
The interval betwixt
my thought and your meaning:
Unmeasured. Uncertain.

I blinked.
My composure
flailed and it faltered.

You continued in speech,
having found your own truth,
having found your own words.

I remain mute.

Endings

On the Hour

tick tock
hands on a clock
to fro
nice and slow
pendulum swings
chime rings
nice and slow
to fro
hands on a clock
tick tock

Writer's Block

The urge strikes;
Write.
I participate.
I create.
But what happens when
Brain and pen
Diverge in thought?
Overwrought,
I frantically try,
Give up, cry.
Paper, bare,
Stares.

Migraine

Like a parched desert, my head
Yearns for the cooling, soothing rain.
Oh, the pain!
The searing, seeking dread.

Two Dimensional

Cardboard cutout people
Are walking down the street.
Cardboard cutout people
Are the only ones I meet.
The world is populated
By these cardboard cutout folk.
Am I the only solid one?
Is this some cosmic joke?
Cardboard cutout people
Mouthing cardboard cutout words,
Cardboard cutout animals
And cardboard cutout birds.
Cardboard cutout buildings
On that cardboard cutout street.
I don't live in two dimensions,
Give me something more concrete!

The Holey Man and the Girl with No Laces

His socks are pulled tight
half-way up his shin
and they tap the floor
instead of his skin

He stares at his phone
as he dances along.
Large headphones keep private
the three/four time song.

The holey man's dirty.
His hair is in dreads.
He's sinew and bone.
His shirt is in threads.

His shoes – they sit neatly;
a pair by the door,
a bag there beside him
laid down on the floor.

And he dances so joyous!
He jumps and he sways
to the three/four time beat
the unknown music plays.

She enters the train car,
clean, upright and pressed,
belying the hobo-chic
way that she's dressed.

Her pant legs have stylish
design-sanded tears.
A baggy shirt covers
the tanktop she wears.

Life Wires

Though her shoes have eyelets
that lace should entwine,
they still seem constructed
laceless by design.

The train car is half-full;
there's seats she can choose.
She sits by the doorway,
right next to his shoes.

The girl with no laces
with laptop on lap
stares straight at the screen
and not at the chap.

The others are watching
but she doesn't dare;
she fears to be caught
in some strange person's stare.

And the holey man beats
his hands next to her ear,
three/four time on plastic –
she's rigid with fear.

But his gaze doesn't touch her.
It's focused within
and his face is serene
as he's into a spin!

And the train car is swaying
But he ne'er skips a beat
as the people around
watch his three/four timed feet.
The train car is slowing
so he slips on his shoes
and he picks up his bag
and he shuts off his muse

The doors then slide open.
The dancing is done.
He departs from the train
And then he is gone.

The girl with no laces
heaves a massive great sigh.
As she closes her laptop,
the girl starts to cry.

"Oh, wasn't he awful?
Why was that allowed?
We should ban all these people!"
she said to the crowd.

"A terror indeed,"
said a man next to me,
"To dance and be happy
when others may see."

Alienation

There's an empty place inside of me,
Somewhere I cannot name.
A shadow deep within
That makes the days all seem the same.
I try to find connections
With the people all around,
But they're different somehow from me
And I feel that I am bound.
My mouth is stopped in silence
And my fingers have been tied,
And they talk a different language
From the one I hear inside.

Asleep in a Car

Drowsy,
I wandered
with weary delight
into the misty
blue-green world
of my dreams.

The city lights shone
in the twilit landscape,
leading me to
places,
times,
and thoughts,
all unknown.

The hum of the bright bigness
surrounded and swallowed
my tiny existence,

and sated,
it too slept.

Moth

Pale wings flutter
Light upon linoleum glares
The wings stutter and start again
Hiccupping their distress
Dying
Dying
Dead

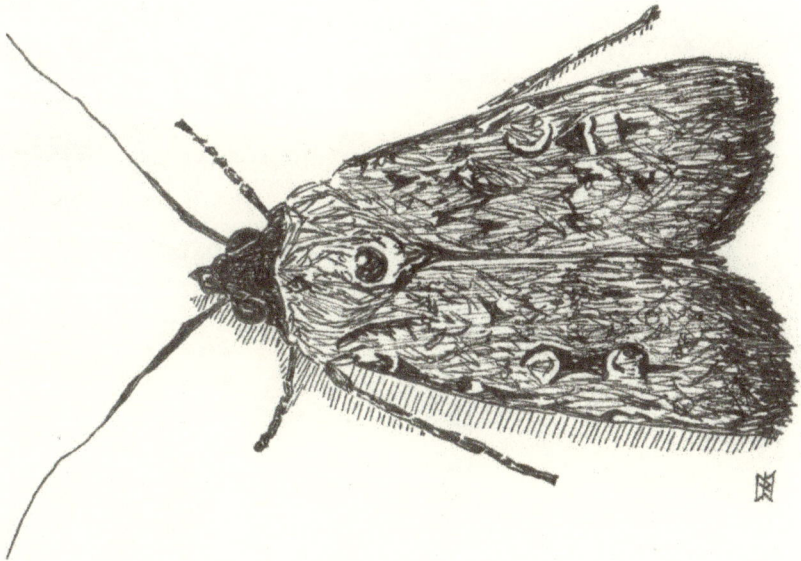

Drizzle

The sky a flat grey-white appears,
waters us with gentle tears.
Hidden in the far off mist,
the scrapers that lie in the dist-
ance. A sighing sad farewell.
So sounds the shadow's parting knell.

Waterbride

Still waters in the night
Show the moon's reflected light
Ripples from a passing breeze
Imitate waves in far off seas
Clear water shows silver fish
Flashing, flick'ring, slightly elfish

Water on flesh is chillingly cold
Covers her flesh and caresses each fold
Naked she enters and deeper she goes
Surrounding herself in the tugs and the flows

Hair in its halo is ribboned with weed
She abases herself to her wet lover's greed
As her from her all privacy slowly is wrung.

She opens her mouth. He enters her lung.

Kristine Sihto

The Astronaut's Lament

i miss the stars
lighting my skies
in faery dust
glow like strings of
diamond ice
i miss the stars
countrified me
now in high rise
paradise a
light on ev'ry
street corner and
i still don't feel
safe at night time
it was diff'rent
once my feet hung
high in the sky
tiptoed on twink-
ling exultant
blackness my mind
soaring in the
magical null
booted feet and
helmeted head
just a thin line
between me and
the infinite
but now i am
old and the stars
are further than
they ever were
twinkling tinsel
lights this city
pretty but not
as beautiful

Life Wires
as what i once
saw from the bub-
ble in space oh
i miss the stars

C

If I could increase my velocity
without acceleration,
harness the days
of soaking in the sun
and ride,
like Apollo,
on light itself,
I could see it all.

But I would still never
reach the edge
of the cone that defines
what is
Real
and what is simply
Potential.

And if I tired of
that eternal chase,
of trying to find
the answer to it all,
if I then slowed
to see the sights,

would I diminish
until
I had never been?

I would like to end
beaming.

·

Poems end, I guess,
with a full stop on the last line
as the words leave the room.

Afterword

I used to keep a journal. Most days found me, for at least an hour or more, pen in hand, book in lap, "Dear Diary..."

I would scribe my days precisely, filling page on page, not with events but with the way that I felt.

That ended.

The first reason is that, when you say, "This is mine; it is just for me..." others will want it. My journals were stolen. My journals were read by surreptitious, greedy eyes. And the things those eyes saw made the thieves angry. My journal was a place I never censored myself. The words were for me and for nobody else, and so, unconcerned with maintaining the cushion of social fictions.

I found I preferred not to know the ugliness of those closest to me when, in anger, they revealed their betrayal. Better to remove that temptation than see that face.

But that is the first reason – there is a second. And that second reason is that I wrote those pages for me, so I read them. Months and years later, I read them. And I found that I did not know the woman who wrote those words. She was a stranger to my older self. Her choices were incomprehensible, her attractions infuriating, her secrets idiotic and her writing was atrocious!

So it is with my poetry. I found, when sorting through my work for Life Wires, that there were voices I no longer recognised. The women who wrote them were strangers, filled with angst and pain. They used poetic structures that were predictable and monotonous, heavy and uninteresting.

I was ruthless. I rejected works that I once thought were brilliant, now too embarrassed to show them in public.

But I tried to keep those voices.

You will hear the voice of the 14-year-old girl in love with Tolkien's poetry in *Cat Dreaming*.

In *Tri Fold* you will hear the devout faith I clung to in my twenties, before the woman I am now rationalised it away.

In *The Breakdown*, you will hear the bitter pain of the woman whose first marriage was destroyed on the one hand by her husband's infidelity, and on the other by her own, deep depression.

I don't claim these works to be good. Many are not. Nor are they soft or easy. I claim them merely to be windows into the experiences of the many women who have worn my face.

And someday, a decade or more into the future, or perhaps tomorrow, I expect that a stranger will look on these words, from eyes that were once mine, and she will think, "I do not know this person. She is a stranger to me."

Notes